Freyr: The Origins and History of the Norse God of Love and Fertility

By Andrew Scott & Charles River Editors

A 20th century depiction of Freyr

About Charles River Editors

Charles River Editors is a boutique digital publishing company, specializing in bringing history back to life with educational and engaging books on a wide range of topics. Keep up to date with our new and free offerings with this 5 second sign up on our weekly mailing list, and visit Our Kindle Author Page to see other recently published Kindle titles.

We make these books for you and always want to know our readers' opinions, so we encourage you to leave reviews and look forward to publishing new and exciting titles each week.

Introduction

A 20ᵗʰ century depiction of Freyr on Odin's throne

Freyr

"Njördr in Nóatún begot afterward two children: the son was called Freyr, and the daughter Freyja; they were fair of face and mighty. Freyr is the most renowned of the Æsir; he rules over the rain and the shining of the sun, and therewithal the fruit of the earth; and it is good to call on him for fruitful seasons and peace."[1]

Much of what is known of the Norse myths comes from

---

[1] Gylfaginning 24

the 10th century onwards. Until this time and, indeed, for centuries afterwards, Norse culture (particularly that of Iceland, where the myths were eventually transcribed) was an oral culture. In fact, in all Scandinavian countries well into the thirteenth century laws were memorized by officials known as "Lawspeakers" who recited them at the "Thing." The Thing was the legislative assembly in Scandinavia "held for judicial purposes."[2]

One of the most famous of these Lawspeakers was the Icelander Snorri Sturluson, a masterful writer who wrote the Prose Edda in the thirteenth century. There are other sources for the Norse myths, namely the later "Poetic Edda," a collection of poems and prose work, and other sagas but the Snorri's Prose Edda is the most complete work whose attribution is known to modern scholars.

The Prose Edda is a collection of Norse Myths split into three sections, the Gylfaginning (the Deluding of Gylfi), the Skáldskaparmál (the Language of Poetry) and the Háttatal (the Enumeration of Meters). The first has a frame story that entails a Swedish King, Gylfi, disguising himself as an old man, Gangleri, when he journeys to Asgard to meet the gods. When he arrives, he meets three men - "High One, Just-As-High, and Third" - who reveal to him stories of the world and the gods. The second section contains a warning for Christians not to believe in

---

[2] Brodeur 1916

the Norse gods, specifically the two families, the Æsir and the Vanir, but also refutes the notion that they were demons, which was a common supposition among some Christians at the time. The Prose Edda begins in this line of thought with a euhemeristic prologue, which traces the history of the Norse Gods as human heroes of Troy, making Thor one of King Priam's sons.

It is believed that Snorri, a Christian, recorded these pagan beliefs so as to preserve and explain the stylistic poetry of Iceland, particularly the popular descriptive devices known as kennings. A kenning is made up of a base word and a modifying word that is used to describe a separate object. For example, "Gold" had a great many kennings, one of which was "Sif's Hair." If, however, the memory of Loki cutting off Sif's hair and replacing it with gold were lost, then this kenning would make no sense to later readers. There are many of these allusions to the myths and it is thanks to them that the myths have survived.

The Norse Myths also appear to follow a chronological narrative, which the historian John Lindow describes as having a "Mythical Past, Present and Future." Loki features in each of these literary "epochs" and it helps to understand the complexity of his character, as well as the belief system, to view the myths in this way.

Freyr was son to sea-god Njördr and twin brother to love goddess Freyja, all of whom were part of the Vanir, a less warlike, divine family. As part of a hostage exchange between warring families, Njördr and Freyr were sent to live with the Æsir. As a member of the Vanir, his integration into the warlike family gave Freyr relatively little to do in surviving mythology. Many of the surviving stories involve Thor exercising his physical strength while Loki and Odin exercise their cunning. Freyr was not noted for either of these attributes, nor did he have a love of besting the Giants, the gods' eternal enemies. Freyr's role as a fertility god—a recurring theme in the Vanir—meant that his relatively rare appearences in the myths weighed heavily on the dominant, cult role he performed across Scandinavia from a surprisingly early time. That being said, there are few superfluous characters in Norse myth, and Freyr is present at two major moments of the gods' history: the union of the two families (although there are very few surviving texts describing this exact moment) and Ragnarök, the apocalyptic end.

Freyr: The Origins and History of the Norse God of Love and Fertility looks at the stories about the legendary Norse deity. Along with pictures depicting important people, places, and events, you will learn about Freyr like never before.

A Note on Norse Names and Letters

Generally speaking, Norse names use the same Latin alphabet as standard English, but there are two unique letters that do not appear in modern English but which are important in Norse mythology. In this text, Norse names will be provided using both this original orthography as well as the Anglicized version.

The first of these letters is /Þ/, which is called "thorn." Thorn appears in Old and Middle English, as well as Old Norse, Icelandic and Gothic alphabets. The sound is similar to the one conveyed in English by /th/. It has been largely abandoned, but it is still used in Iceland and appears in the Icelandic texts that are the primary sources of information about Thor.

The second letter is /ð/, which is called "eth." Eth was used in Old English, the Medieval Scandinavian languages, and is still used in Icelandic and Faeroese (the language of the Faeroe Islands located near Iceland). Eth also conveys a sound similar to /th/, and in Old English it was interchangeable with thorn, but in some Scandinavian forms, it is a silent letter. These letters are used for historical accuracy, but most readers will be better off utilizing the Anglicized names. Thus, readers should know that Thor's daughter's "real" name is "Þrúðr," but in English she is typically called "Thrud."

Origins and Sources

"Gangleri began his questioning thus: 'Who is foremost, or oldest, of all the gods?' Hárr answered: 'He is called in our speech Allfather, but in the Elder Ásgard he had twelve names: one is Allfather; the second is Lord, or Lord of Hosts; the third is Nikarr, or Spear-Lord; the fourth is Nikudr, or Striker; the fifth is Knower of Many Things; the sixth, Fulfiller of Wishes; the seventh, Far-Speaking One; the eighth, The Shaker, or He that Putteth the Armies to Flight;   the ninth, The Burner; the tenth, The Destroyer; the eleventh, The Protector; the twelfth, Gelding.'" - *The Gylfaginning III, from the Prose Edda.*[3]

Throughout the millennia, a lot of different gods have been worshipped by different cultures and civilizations, and many of them have fascinated even those who read about them without believing in them. But one often overlooked aspect of the various gods is the similarities some of them tend to share with each other, almost unquestionably a result of the fact that cultures interacted with each other via trade, war, and other forms of communication. Thus, it should not come as a surprise

---

3   Text available here: http://www.sacred-texts.com/neu/pre/pre04.htm

that the Christian God shares similarities with other ancient deities among neighboring civilizations in the Near East, and it's readily apparent that the Romans co-opted their mythology almost entirely from the Greeks.

The Norse gods were descended from a religious tradition often referred to as "Indo-European," which includes the pantheons of ancient Europe, including the Greeks, Romans, Celts, Germans, Slavs, etc. "Indo-European" is a term not for cultures but for language families, great groupings of languages that share a historical root even as they have diverged greatly over their histories. Indo-European languages include all of the Western European languages, the languages of Iran, and those of Northern India. This is a sweeping generalization, and there are a number of exceptions. For example, Basque, Turkish, Finnish, Estonian, Saami and Hungarian are not Indo-European despite the fact many of the peoples speaking these languages reside in Europe. This is particularly important when discussing mythology and gods because it is important not to automatically associate language family with culture. The traditional Saami and Finnish pantheons had great similarities with those of the Norse, including their own versions of Thor, despite wide language differences.

Generally, the "Indo-European" religion is associated with the language groups, but this religious system, which took many forms in different regions, was worshiped by other groups of people who did not speak Indo-European languages. Indeed, there is nothing inherent in speaking an Indo-European language that makes one predisposed to follow their gods, as evidenced by the fact that huge numbers of Indo-European speakers today follow the Semitic god of the Christians, Muslims and Jews.

When coming across such similarities between the gods of different cultures, there are only three logical explanations for the similarities. The first is parallel evolution, meaning the same outside force led people in different contexts to develop similar ideas. The second is a common origin, meaning that the two different but somewhat similar concepts both came from the same historical roots. Finally, the third option is diffusion, an idea that was developed in one culture and was then exported to other societies.

In the case of these gods, when researchers cannot establish historical contact between two peoples who have gods that only share a few similarities, they generally assume the reason is parallel evolution. For instance, Thor and the Christian Jehovah were probably both partially inspired by the same awe at the natural phenomenon of thunder and lightning. However, in circumstances where the cultures in question have shared historical contacts, such as trade or war, then the idea of independent development becomes far less likely. For example, in the case of the thunder gods of Europe, there have long been discussions about the relationships between them, and one school of thought has promoted the idea that these gods in fact emerge from a single historical deity.

One of the methods used by scholars is the use of historical linguistics to reconstruct words. Historical linguists take related ("cognate") words in related languages and attempt to trace them back to the original root word that they descend from. This is more complex than a simple comparison, as it also involves taking into account how sounds shift over time. When there are more cognate words available, the search for the root becomes progressively easier, and (theoretically) the results become more accurate and can have a greater time depth. At the same time, unfortunately, the results are always hypothetical, since it's impossible to be sure how the speakers of a dead language spoke. Thus, the products of these studies, the proposed ancient words, are always marked in scholarship with an asterisk "*" to note that they cannot be confirmed.

*Þunraz (pronounced "*thunraz") is just such a word. Scholars took various terms, including the gods Thor (or, as the word is sometimes written, "Þórr"), Donar, Donner, and Þunor, but they also looked at cognate terms like "thunder" (English), "dunder" (Swedish), "donder" (Dutch), "tornden" (Danish), "donner" (German) and "þrumuveðri" (Icelandic). Scholars who traced backwards from these words to reconstruct *Þunraz argue that the word was probably both the term for the god and for the natural phenomenon of thunder. *Þunraz would be an ancient, early Indo-European god, one of the archetypes which the other pantheons drew upon, altered, and mixed with currents from other cultures to create the various gods that can be accounted for in the historic record.[4]

There are few natural forces that are both awe inspiring and simultaneously everyday as thunder and it should be no surprise that when the heavens rumbled for our ancestors, they often heard the voice of gods. This is not a uniquely pagan concept, as Christians also imagine their God as ruling from the heavens and his voice as thunder, for instance in Psalm 29:3-9, which reads in part, "The voice of the LORD is over the waters; the God of glory thunders, the LORD thunders over the mighty waters.| The voice of the LORD is powerful; the voice of the LORD is majestic. | The voice of the LORD breaks the cedars [...] The voice of the LORD strikes with flashes of lightning.| The voice of the LORD shakes the desert [...] The voice of the LORD twists the oaks and strips the forests bare. And in his temple all cry, 'Glory!'"

---

4 *Patterns in Comparative Religion* (1974) by Mircea Eliade

However similar their power over thunder and lightning, Jehovah and Thor do not seem to share a common origin, as Jehovah descends from the Semitic tradition of today's Near East. Historically, Jehovah is linked to deities like El and Enil, whereas Thor is descended from the Indo-European religious tradition, which includes the pantheons of ancient Europe, notably the Greeks, Romans, Celts, Germans, Slavs, etc.

Thor was not the only thunder god found amongst the Indo-Europeans; in fact, it was a common trope found across the religions. Similar gods included *Zeus* (Ancient Greek), Jupiter/Jove (Ancient Roman), Taranis (Celtic), Donar/Donner (German), Þunor (Saxon), Perun (Slav), Perkūnas (Baltic peoples), Ukko (Finnish), and Horagalles (Saami). Some of these gods are quite obviously similar to Thor. Donar was a god not only of thunder but also of war and strength who was worshiped by the Teutonic peoples, the predecessors of today's Germans. Similarly, Þunor (pronounced "Thunor") amongst the Saxons, Thuner amongst the Frisians (of today's northern Netherlands) and ðunor (again pronounced "Thunor") of the Old English, all bear great similarities to Thor. For example, they were also associated with oak trees and sacred groves, such as the one dedicated to Donar that Saint Boniface chopped down in the modern-day German state of Hesse in the 720s.[5]

Conversely, Jupiter and Zeus share many similarities with each other, as do most Roman and Greek gods, but they are quite different from Thor/Donar/Thunor. Zeus and Jupiter are not monster-fighting warriors associated with forest groves but instead kingly gods whose position atop sacred mountains allows them to reign over all of creation. While Zeus and Jupiter are known to fling lightning bolts, they leave the hand-to-hand to gods like Ares/Mars.

Somewhere in between are the gods Taranis, Perun, and Perkūnas. Taranis was worshiped by the Celts of Gaul and appears to be a god of fire. He was associated with both lightning and the sun, and it was said that his followers made ritual sacrifices by burning their victims in constructions made of wickerwork. Taranis is mostly known today through the writings of Roman observers, particularly Julius Caesar.[6] The Slavic Perun is king of the gods, like Jupiter and Zeus, but he is also a mighty warrior who fights monsters with either an axe or a hammer and is associated with a sacred oak tree.[7] Perkūnas, worshiped by the ancient Lithuanians, was a similar god, also connected to oaks and hills[8].

5 "St. Boniface" in *The New Catholic Encyclopedia* accessed online at
   http://www.newadvent.org/cathen/02656a.htm
6 "Taranis" in *Encyclopedia Britannica* accessed online at
   http://global.britannica.com/EBchecked/topic/583342/Taranis
7 *Perun: God of Thunder* (2003) by Mark Yoffe and Joseph Krafczik. Peter Lang Publishers.
8 "Lithuanian Mythology" by Gintaras Beresnevicius, accessed online at
   http://www.crvp.org/book/Series04/IVA-17/chapter_iv.htm, published by the Lithuanian Institute of
   Culture and Arts

For centuries, observers have discussed the roots of religious belief and deities, and historically there have been three major schools of thought which have sought to explain the existence of the traditional pantheons, specifically those of Greece, Rome, the Norse and the Near East. These schools are the Euhermist, Historicist and Psychological, all of which seek to explain not just the religious aspects but also the history and secular nature of the religions. What they share is a respect for the believers of those past eras, and these schools attempt to show how people could have rationally believed in the existence of these gods and have found meaning in their lives from them.

Unfortunately, the ultimate answer to the question of the roots of Germanic Heathenism will never be entirely clear, because these peoples did not write. This means scholars are limited to three imperfect sources of information: the surviving myths, historical linguistics and archeology. Each of these three suffer from something known as a "preservation bias", a term used in archeology to explain that some materials preserve well (like stone and ceramic) while others do not (like cloth or wood). This means that when scholars look back at ancient peoples, they are apt to discover more about the finest stone tool makers than about the finest ancient weavers or woodcarvers.

Furthermore, information is not maintained perfectly among any of these sources. Instead it is spotty and has major gaps. For instance, archaeology can explain quite a bit about ancient peoples' food, housing and technology, but little about their stories, myths and music. Historical linguistics can explain the ancient relationships between peoples and something about their movements, comparative mythology can provide insight about belief systems, but neither creates a perfect picture. The past is always murky, and this means that while people may favor one explanation about the origins of the gods over another, they can never argue from a position of perfect certainty.

The Euhemerists are named after an early Christian figure named Euhemerus, who theorized that the Greek pantheon was in fact the deification of long-dead war leaders. Euhermerus argued that the Greek deities were in fact ancient human kings and heroes transformed into gods through the process of centuries of retelling and exaggeration. The Euhemerist position was a common one taken by early Christian polemicists fighting against Greek and Roman paganism, and it was well-known to any Medieval European Christian scholar, especially those who studied (and argued against) the Norse Heathen pantheon.9

---

9 "Euhemerism: A Mediaeval Interpretation of Classical Paganism," John Daniel Cooke, in the journal *Speculum*, Vol. 2, No. 4, Oct., 1927, p. 397

Ancient statue of Euhemerus

The early Christian Norse scholars began to use Euhemerism as an argument against the Heathens, and the two most important writers in this area were Saxo Grammaticus and Snorri Sturluson, the author of the *Prose Edda*.[10] Snorri proposed his Euhemerist theory in the *Prose Edda* when he explained his belief that Odin and Thor and the other gods were once mortal humans, and that the sites of their tombs became places of worship over the centuries. Snorri believed that the Aesir were a group of people who lived in a city called Asgard in Western Asia and that their king - Odin - led them westward into the Germanic lands to found a new

10 "Saxo Grammaticus" (2012). In *Britannica Concise Encyclopedia*. Retrieved from http://www.credoreference.com.libezproxy2.syr.edu/entry/ebconcise/saxo_grammaticus

kingdom.

18ᵗʰ century manuscript of Snorri's *Prose Edda*

The Euhemerist authors of the early Christian and Medieval period had reason to believe that ancient kings would set themselves up as gods, and that they might be worshiped by their descendents. After all, they could simply point to the Roman Emperors. The Imperial Cult was the state religion of Rome between the founding of the Empire and its conversion to Christianity, and emperors were said to have divine guidance and, after their death, could be elevated to godhood by a vote in the Roman Senate. Some Romans who were elevated in this way included Julius Caesar and his heir Augustus. It served as a crucial element in holding the Roman Empire together, and it was bitterly opposed by the Early Christians. They could point to the human origins of Caesar and Augustus, and no doubt it was easy to theorize there was a similar explanation for the deification of gods like Zeus and Odin.[11]

In a similar vein, it's possible that actual historical figures were integrated into mythology. For example, Achilles may not have actually fought at Troy, but historians are virtually certain there was a Trojan War, and it would make sense for the figures in Homer's *Iliad* to be based off actual stories of the war that at least had some basis in fact. There is, however, little direct evidence that suggests pantheons of gods were based on actual historical figures.

Thus, this theory about actual historical figures probably does not explain the origins of the Norse gods, at least not comprehensively. The Norse gods of the late Pre-

---

11 "Imperial Cult." (1999). In *Late Antiquity: A Guide to the Postclassical World.* Retrieved from http://www.credoreference.com.libezproxy2.syr.edu/entry/hupla/imperial_cult

Christian era have direct links to deities from across Northern Europe, and over a vast period of time. Naturally, this means theories about the origins of the Norse Heathen pantheon have a habit of paralleling interest in Paganism more generally.

  For many centuries, interest in the Norse gods lay dormant, but it was rekindled in the 19th century during the Romantic Movement. Germans became interested in folklore, and with that came a scholarly interest in the roots of the German language and ancient Germanic culture. The earliest linguists like the Grimm brothers (the ones of fairy tale fame) sought to compare surviving remnants of various German dialects and folk traditions and then use a comparative approach to slowly trace backwards and find the shared common roots of what are today disparate languages and cultures. This technique was applied not only to languages but also to religious belief. By collecting the fragments of folklore and written tales and comparing them across regions, an understanding of the earlier forms could be made, and they did the same with the names of the gods. For example, the Norse "Odin" is joined by a number of other Germanic gods with similar names: the Old English "Wōden", Old Saxon "Wôdan" and Old High German "Wôtan." Using these names, as well as their understanding of how languages have evolved and what types of sound changes are the most common, historical linguists have argued that the original Germanic god in the language they call "Proto-Germanic" was known as "*Wodanaz" or "*Wōđanaz." The asterisk (*) is used in historical linguistics to denote a word for which scholars have no confirmation but is a hypothetical reconstruction.

The "Psychological" approach endeavors to explain the forms of religious belief - particularly legends - by explaining them as localized manifestations of universal human psychological impulses. The roots of this approach come from the late 19th century, but it fully flowered in the early 20th century. In 1902, William James published *The Varieties of Religious Experience*, which explored the nature of religious belief from a psychological perspective, trying to uncover exactly how people's psychological needs fuel various forms of religious experiences.

Building on pioneers like James, the works of psychoanalysts like Freud and Jung explored the power of the unconscious mind. Jung especially examined the concept of "archetypes", and the powerful influence that these figures have upon on people's minds. Myths and gods can be interpreted within this framework as psychological tools societies have created to assist in navigating their crises.

One important concept that Jung examined that has

particular relevance on a study of Odin is the idea of the "psychopomp." In mythology, a psychopomp is the figure who delivers the souls of the dead from the land of the living to the afterlife. But Jung pushed further and explained that psychopomps were also mediators between the conscious and unconscious parts of people's minds. These figures are sometimes animals, like ravens (who have a special connection to Odin), sometimes human, like shamans who assist the spiritual journeys of their flocks, and sometimes mythical human-like beings, such as Odin. Odin is a perfect example of a Jungian psychopomp, as he navigates not only life and death but also the worlds of the seen and unseen, between magic and reality. He is a god of prophecy, and, like the shaman, his insight into the hidden realm provides insight into the future.

  While the three schools do have some similarities, in the end they provide very different explanations for the existence of Odin and similar gods. Was he a human king misguidedly deified by his followers? Was he part of an ancient folktale that has been morphed and melded with other tales over the centuries? Was he simply a psychological tool created to help people address and make sense of events in their own lives? The truth may be somewhere in the middle, with true historical figures providing some of the fodder and being welded to ancient tales and folklore.

Freyr, Sweden, and Elsewhere

A Gotland runestone believed to depict Odin, Thor, and Freyr

In Norse myth, Odin's Æsir had a great war with another divine family, the Vanir. When peace was made, hostages were exchanged and marriage vows were made to ensure the gods never went to war with each other again. In the *Ynglinga Saga*, the Vanir are transformed into the "people of Vanaland", but the war plays out in much the same way, featuring the same characters portrayed as mortals so as to not offend contemporary Christian sensibilities.[12]

---

[12] Simek 2007

One of these denizens of Vanaland is Frey, son of Njord, who became sovereign when Odin died. Sturlson suggests the Swedes believed Odin did not die but simply traveled back to "ancient Asgaard". This led to their belief in Odin as a god.

Freyr appears as a great warrior and prosperous ruler in the *Ynglinga Saga,* as this prosperity and greatness were his main attributes from a very early, pre-Christian tradition, firmly rooted not in Asia or Asaland but in northern Europe and Sweden in particular. "Frey took the kingdom after Njord, and was called *drot* by the Swedes, and they paid taxes to him. He was, like his father, fortunate in friends and in good seasons. Frey built a great temple at Upsal, made it his chief seat, and gave it all his taxes, his land, and goods. Then began the Upsal domains, which have remained ever since. Then began in his days the peace of Fróði; and then there were good seasons, in all the land, which the Swedes ascribed to Frey, so that he was more worshipped than the other gods, as the people became much richer in his days by reason of the peace and good seasons. His wife was called Gerðr, daughter of Gymis, and their son was called Fjölnir. Frey was called by another name, Yngvi; and this name Yngvi was considered long after in his race as a name of honour, so that his descendants have since been called Ynglinger. Frey fell into a sickness; and as his illness took the upper hand, his men took the plan of letting few approach him. In the meantime they raised a great mound, in which they placed a door with three holes in it. Now, when Frey died they bore him secretly into the mound, but told the Swedes he was alive; and they kept watch over him for three years. They brought all the taxes into the mound, and through the one hole they put in the gold, through the other the silver, and through the third the copper money that was paid. Peace and good seasons continued."[13]

The above quote comes from the euhemeristic *Ynglinga Saga*. It tells the story of Freyr's terrestrial beginnings, but within those lines lie an interesting history of the god. Firstly, the connection Freyr had with Sweden in particular is undisputed. Many sacrifices to Freyr are recorded in the literature and it appears he was especially popular in East Sweden, since there are numerous cult place-names connected with him.[14]

Writing during the second half of the 11th century CE, the chronicler, Adam of Bremen, catalogued the deeds of the Bishops of Hamburg, and in doing so, sheds fascinating light on Freyr. Notably, he describes the major cult temple at Uppsala dedicated to Thor as *Wodan* and Fricco. More will be said about Fricco in the coming chapter, but it is sufficient to say here that this is the name

_____

[13] Ynglinga Saga 10
[14] Simek 2007

Adam of Bremen gave to Freyr, and his account of the temple shows that Freyr held a very high position in the Norse pantheon, alongside Odin (Wodan) and Thor.

A depiction of Freyr constructing the Temple at Uppsala

A depiction of the inside of the temple

  The Yngling kings mentioned here are the dynasty of
kings that began their reign in Sweden and later expanded
outward to Norway, and who counted the god Freyr as
their ancester. The name "Yngvi" is connected with other
names credited to Freyr, those of Yngvi-Freyr or
Ingunarfreyr Ynglings (found only in the Eddic poem
"Lokasenna").[15] Out of this dynasty came the first
Norwegian king, Harald Fairhair (died ca. 933 CE), whose
lineage can be traced to as late as the 14th century CE. The
Swedish Yngling dynasty, however, has a genealogy
whose beginnings were written down by poets in the 9th

---

[15] ibid.

century CE and then later by Sturlson in his *Ynglinga Saga*. The original meaning of Yngvi is uncertain, but there is a strong likelihood it came from the Germanic god Ingwaz, who was also the mythical ancestor of the Ingaevones tribe mentioned by the 1st century CE Roman historian, Tacitus, in his *Germania*. Given the geographical and cultural proximity of the Ingaevones and the Swedes, Yngvi-Freyr most likely has a long tradition connecting him with *Ingwia-fraujaz,* meaning "lord of the Ingaevones". If this is the case, then Freyr's place as a mythical ancestor to Northern European peoples would go back at least as far as the Roman period.

The "Peace of Fróði" mentioned in the *Ynglinga Saga* is a very important event in Freyr's biography. Firstly, historians have long accepted Fróði and Freyr as being identical characters with different names, although the only surviving attestations of this connection are in Sturlson's *Ynglinga Saga*. Nevertheless, this peace is first mentioned in a 10th century CE poem and refers to legendary Danish King Fróði, whose reign coincided with a series of good harvests and a greater sense of security than had been felt before. The prosperity of the Danish people was said to have been so abundant that nobody would steal a golden ring if it were left out in the open. This time of peace is akin to the common occurrence of a golden age in cultural memory across the globe. These golden ages often consist of unprecedented peace and an abundance of food, the likes of which struggling generations looked back at with envy. Attributing peace and abundance to a king was a common way to date the phenomenon, and this may be the reason behind the connection between Fróði and Freyr, since a king whose reign was associated with good harvests was considered blessed by the fertility deity who, in this case, was Freyr/Yngvi. Both Sturlson and the 12th and 13th century CE Christian grammarian Saxo would eventually date this period to the reign of Augustus and the birth of Jesus Christ, further adding to the "golden age" attribution of the leader-deity.[16]

Freyr's dominion was not limited to Sweden. Both he and Njördr, his father, were often invoked alongside Odin and Thor, the beloved Æsir gods. One such example of this is when Freyr appears in the oath "so help me Freyr and Njördr and *hinn almáttki áss* [almighty god]", a common exclamation across Scandinavia. Furthermore, in Norway, it is believed that *jarls* gave the first sacrificial libation to Odin and subsequent ones to Njördr and Freyr.[17]

In Iceland, *Freysgoði* appears in the historical record as a common title for "priest of Freyr". A late, Icelandic saga, *Vatnsdoela Saga,* mentions one such priest who carried an

---

[16] ibid.
[17] ibid.

image of Freyr in a bag, substantiated by archaeological finds of such artifacts.[18] These finds, especially those from the Viking-Age (ca. 8th-11th centuries CE), took the form of phallic statuettes, such as those found in Rällinge, Sweden.[19] According to Book 1 of the Danish grammarian Saxo's *Gesta Danorum,* "prehistoric" Danish King Hadingus established an annual sacrifice to Freyr, thus exemplifying the spread of Freyr's cult from its likely origins in Sweden, as well as the fervor with which he was worshipped.[20]

There is also the story of a pair of statues of two, wooden men taken from a burial mound sacred to Freyr in Sweden. As the story goes, one of the statues was kept in Sweden whereas the other was taken westward to Norway. This is a typical story, explaining the migration of a cult, substantiated by the archaeological evidence. As far as Iceland, place-names are recorded that suggest the cult of Freyr was practised west of Sweden. Many Icelandic sagas preserve the memory of these worshippers in stories of horses sacred to the god, early accounts of weapons being forbidden in Freyr's temples, and of the unfortunate men of Iceland who had either forsaken Freyr's worship or did not respect his horses or his temples.[21]

---

[18] ibid.
[19] ibid.
[20] Lindow 2001
[21] Ellis Davidson 1990

A Viking statuette believed to depict Freyr

Fertility

In contrast with Æsir's destructive force, the lesser known Vanir's function seems to have been that of preserving peace and fertility in the world,[22] and Freyr's fertility and agricultural cult stands in marked contrast to Odin's battle cult.[23] Sturlson refers to Freyr as "god of the world", hinting that Freyr's relative absence from many dramatic stories in his *Edda* is not indicative of the power he and his sister Freyja wielded from a mythological and cult perspective.[24]

Adam of Bremen corroborates the connection between

---

[22] ibid.
[23] ibid.
[24] ibid.

Freyr and marriage when he describes the cult images of him being either phallic in shape or replete with phallic symbolism. Adam refers to him as "Fricco", saying he was portrayed *cum ingenti priapo* (with a huge phallus). Fricco's etymology has yet to be fully agreed upon, but it is likely a Latinized term for Freyr, coming from *friðkan*

In the Icelandic manuscript of sagas and history, *Flateyjarbók*, there is the story of a fugitive Icelander, Ögmund, who flees from the royal court of Norway because he is falsely accused of murder.[25] When he arrives in Sweden, he meets a priestess of Freyr who pulls a statue of the god around on a cart or a wagon. Ögmund finds a demon—or Freyr, the god according to other accounts—occupying the statue and manages to expel it from both the statue and the cart by invoking the god of the Norwegian court. After this, Ögmund pretends that he is the god himself. He mounts the wagon and the people of Sweden—who are apparently very credulous—are exuberant when their god not only agrees to take part in their meals but also gladly accepts their gifts of gold and fine clothing. When the priestess miraculously becomes pregnant, it confirms the "god's" powers as a fertility deity. Out of this story, many scholars have extrapolated a version of Freyr-worship as that of a travelling god, most likely paraded atop a wagon in a kind of procession,

---

[25] Lindow 2001

bestowing health and abundance on all those in his favor. The female assistant who accompanied the cart—known as the wife of Freyr—soon became pregnant, which adds credibility to the claim that Ögmund was the fertility god personified. In Sweden, the character of Freyr's wife was enacted in the procession by a priestess of Freyr's great temple at Uppsala.[26]

Furthermore, it seems the people of Sweden believed their kings had a power akin to that of Freyr's ability to bring peace and abundance to the land. Since many of their deaths appear to have been violent ones, some scholars believe the deaths to have been ceremonial or sacrificial at some point in history.[27] This may have something to do with the curious association the Vanir had with human sacrifice, though little more than speculation can be made by historians in this respect.

Death

Freyr was associated with fertility, but he was also associated with death and burial. According to the euhemeristic *Ynglinga Saga*, the man-Freyr's death remained a secret for three years. Kept in a burial mound during this time, propitiary gifts were made to him via a door and three holes that had been bored into the mound.[28]

---

[26] Frazer 1922
[27] Ellis Davidson 1990
[28] ibid.

This may go some way toward explaining the cult practise of dedicating propitiary offerings to Freyr by burying them in mounds.

One of Freyr's other motifs, that of the ship, was also intrinsically connected with death. Since the Bronze Age, ships have been used in funeral ceremonies in a variety of ways, not the least of which was the act of burying aristocratic members of society along with their finest possessions and a ship, often built expressly for the purpose. An excellent example of this is the ship discovered at the beginning of the 20th century in Oseberg, Norway, which contained the bodies of two women alongside their valuables.

Magical Objects

How Freyr received two of the three magical objects associated with him forms part of one of the most well-known and beloved stories in Norse mythology. Sturlson recounts the episode in his *Skáldskaparmál* when he asks the poetic question: "Why is gold called Sif's Hair?" The question is a record of one of the kennings used for gold during Sturlson's lifetime, the answer to which indicates what makes Norse mythology so fascinating: dwarves, treasures, magical objects associated with the gods, and the genesis of the symbolism as a result Loki's meddling.

"Loki, for mischief's sake, cut off all [of Thor's

wife] Sif's hair. But when Thor learned of this, he seized Loki, and would have broken every bone in him, had he not sworn to get the Black Elves to make Sif hair of gold, such that it would grow like other hair. After that, Loki went to those dwarves who are called Ívaldi's Sons; and they made the hair, and Skíðblaðnir also, and the spear, which became Odin's possession, and was called Gungnir.

"Then Loki wagered his head with the dwarf called Brokkr that Brokkr's brother Sindri could not make three other precious things equal in virtue to these. Now when they came to the smithy, Sindri laid a pigskin in the hearth and bade Brokkr blow, and did not cease work until he took out of the hearth that which he had laid therein. But when he went out of the smithy, while the other dwarf was blowing, straightway a fly settled upon his hand and stung: yet he blew on as before, until the smith took the work out of the hearth; and it was a boar, with mane and bristles of gold. Next, he laid gold in the hearth and bade Brokkr blow and cease not from his blast until he should return. He went out; but again the fly came and settled on Brokkr's neck, and bit now half again as hard as before; yet he blew even until the smith took from the hearth that gold ring which is called Draupnir. Then Sindri laid iron in the hearth and bade him blow, saying that it would be spoiled if the blast failed. Straightway the fly settled between Brokkr's eyes and stung his eyelid, but when the blood fell into his eyes so that he could not see, then he clutched at it with his hand as swiftly as he could, while the bellows grew flat, and he swept the fly from him. Then the smith came thither and said that it had come near to spoiling all that was in the hearth. Then he took from the forge a hammer, put all the precious works into the hands of Brokkr his brother, and bade him go with them to Ásgard and claim the wager.

"Now when he and Loki brought forward the precious gifts, the Æsir sat down in the seats of judgment; and that verdict was to prevail which Odin, Thor, and Freyr should render. Then Loki gave Odin the spear Gungnir, and to Thor the hair which Sif was to have, and Skíðblaðnir to Freyr, and told the virtues of all these things: that the spear would never stop in its thrust; the hair would grow to the flesh as soon as it came upon Sif's head; and Skíðblaðnir would have a favoring breeze as soon as the sail was raised, in whatsoever direction it might go, but could be folded together like a napkin and be kept in Freyr's pouch if he so desired.

   "Then Brokkr brought forward his gifts: he gave to Odin the ring, saying that eight rings of the same weight would drop from it every ninth night; to Freyr he gave the boar, saying that it could run through air and water better than any horse, and it could never become so dark with night or gloom of the Murky Regions that there should not be sufficient light where be went, such was the glow from its mane and bristles.

   "Then he gave the hammer to Thor, and said that Thor might smite as hard as he desired, whatsoever might be before him, and the hammer would not fail; and if he threw it at anything, it would never miss, and never fly so far as not to return to his hand; and if be desired, he might keep it in his sark, it was so small; but indeed it was a flaw in the hammer that the fore-haft was somewhat short.

   "This was their decision: that the hammer was best of all the precious works, and in it there was the greatest defense against the Rime-Giants; and they gave sentence, that the dwarf should have his wager."[29]

Unsurprisingly, Loki does not lose his head in the wager. Employing cunning once he was caught by Thor and taken back to the dwarf, he tells his would-be attacker that he agreed to give him his head but not his neck. Realizing the impossibility of not harming the neck while decapitating the god, the dwarf withdraws and Loki lives another day.

What is especially important about this episode is that Freyr is mentioned as being one of the three most important gods in Norse mythology. By receiving his gifts along with Odin and Thor, Freyr's exalted position is established. Moreover, he receives two gifts during the same episode in which the most important object, arguably a symbol of Norse, pre-Christian beliefs, also appeared: Thor's hammer, Mjölnir. The use of this symbol continued well into the Christian era[30] as a symbol of protection of humankind and the gods. Nowhere is this more evident than in the Norse myths, since the gods only ever seemed to come under real threat when Thor was away using his hammer on Giants, though he was always on-hand to return in time to fight off the threat.

---

[29] Skáldskáparmál 35
[30] Lindow 2001

The Skog Church Tapestry, which is believed to depict Odin, Thor, and Freyr

Gullinborsti translates as "golden mane and/or bristle", its luminescense no doubt playing a part in Freyr's association with the sun, and subsequently, the seasons. Historically, the boar has also been connected with fertility and the Swedish royal house in particular, further establishing the connection between this house and Freyr.[31] Both Freyr and his sister Freyja were associated with the boar, too, but while Freyr's was Gullinborsti—whose mane or bristles were symbolically significant and well-attested in surviving literature—very little is known about Freyja's boar, named Hildisvin.

In both early Sweden and Anglo-Saxon England, the boar was an extremely symbolic animal, having been found either stamped onto—or crafted into—many ceremonial objects from the period as well as weapons and armor. In Anglo-Saxon times, the boar was believed to have possessed protective powers, as noted in the 10th century poem, *Beowulf,* in which a boar attached to a helmet was said to keep guard over the life of the warrior wearing it.[32] Even though the Vanir were not a warlike family of gods, they did offer protection, which would have included protection over an act of war if the boar were given an emblematic place of pride.[33]

Aside from what is said in the *Skáldskáparmál*, Sturlson elaborates on Freyr's ship, putting a question about it into Gylfi's mouth in the *Gylfaginning*. Although there is a much more ominous tone in this section when discussing the greatest ships of the Norse worlds:

---

[31] Simek 2007
[32] Ellis Davidson 1990
[33] ibid.

"Then said Gangleri: 'What is to be said of *Skíðblaðnir*, that which is best of ships? Is there no ship equally great?'

"Hárr replied: '*Skíðblaðnir* is best of ships and made with most skill of craftsmanship; but Naglfar is the largest ship; Müspell has it. Certain dwarves, sons of Ívaldi, made *Skíðblaðnir* and gave the ship to Freyr. It is so great that all the Æsir may man it, with their weapons and armaments, and it has a favoring wind as soon as the sail is hoisted, whithersoever it is bound; but when there is no occasion for going to sea in it, it is made of so many things and with so much cunning that then it may be folded together like a napkin and kept in one's pouch.'"[34]

---

[34] Gylfaginning 43

A 20th century depiction of the ship

Like many magical objects, *Skíðblaðnir* is capable of operating on its own and is not subject to the limitations and whims of nature. In the *Gylfaginning*, however, it is contrasted with the largest ship known to the gods, *Naglfar*. The "Müspell" to which Sturlson refers is a reference to the Fire-World where Surtr lives and from whence he will lead all forces of evil against the gods at Ragnarök. By contrasting the size of Freyr's ship with *Naglfar*, Sturlson once more records the looming victory of evil over good.

In general, the Vanir have long been associated with ships and seafaring, even in their cult practice, so it is unsurprising that Freyr would be the owner of a magical vessel such as *Skíðblaðnir*.[35] There is a long tradition of ships being carried in processions in northern Europe, and it is believed said ships may have even folded up when not in use, giving birth to one of *Skíðblaðnir*'s more fanciful charactistics. In fact, many of these ceremonial ships were kept inside churches in Scandinavia, right up to modern times. In Denmark, there was also the tradition of using ships to bless the fields so that they may yield abundance. Given that there was often a fertile field located next to a temple of Freyr, these two cult characteristics—the field and the ship used to bless it— are clearly associated with the god of fertility.[36]

Freyr's sword was one of his important objects and possibly pivotal to the ultimate survival of the gods at Ragnarök. However, very little is known about it, including its name. There is a long tradition in Northern European history and myth of giving names to swords, such as Beowulf's sword, Hrunting. Freyr's sword, which was apparently capable of fighting on its own as long as it was wielded by a "worthy" person, plays a part in myths

[35] Simek 2007
[36] Ellis Davidson 1990

and sagas. It's possible that, since Freyr was not part of the bellicose Æsir, less emphasis was placed on the sword than, for instance, Thor's hammer, Mjölnir. Thor's hammer was the sign of his protection of the gods and mortals, while Freyr's sword was the symbol of a very costly mistake.

"And Álfheimr the gods

to Freyr once gave

As a tooth-gift in ancient times."[37]

The above quote comes from a stanza of the Eddic poem, *Grímnismál*, briefly mentioning Freyr's home, Álheimr, given to him by (presumably) the rest of the Vanir gods when he got his first tooth. Giving a child a gift on the advent of their first tooth was evidently a common practice in Scandinavia, as it is to this day.[38]

The land where the "Light-Elves" lived is described by Sturlson in the *Gylfaginning* as follows: "That which is called Álfheimr is one, where dwell the peoples called Light-Elves; but the Dark-Elves dwell down in the earth, and they are unlike in appearance, but by far more unlike in nature. The Light-Elves are fairer to look upon than the sun, but the Dark-Elves are blacker than pitch."[39]

---

[37] Grímnismál 5
[38] Bellows 1936
[39] Gylfaginning 17

Historically, Álfheimr was the name for the non-mythic region between Norway and Sweden. The royal dynasty of this region claimed their descent from the Norwegian Ynglingr Harald Fairhair. Their people were described as being exceptionally beautiful, which is one possible reason for their association with the Light-Elves.[40]

Given that Harald Fairhair was descended from the Ynglings and therefore considered Yngvi-Freyr an ancestor, the association with the terrestrial geography of Álfheimr and Freyr is unsurprising. That the people of the area were considered beautiful also coincides with the belief that Freyr—and his twin sister, Freyja—were extremely beautiful, too, further cementing Freyr's reputation as the divinity of Álfheimr, both celestial and terrestrial. CELESTIAL / TERRESTRIAL

The Wooing of Gerðr

A picture of gold pieces believed to depict Freyr and

[40] Simek 2007

Gerðr

This episode is Freyr's main narrative in all of Norse myth, and despite the fact that it would come to define him, he plays a surprisingly passive role.[41]

It is for lack of a better term that most historians describe Gerðr 's request, barter, and ultimate threatening as "wooing", but it is nevertheless a record of a bleaker time in which such actions were more accepted. The episode concerning Gerðr takes place in Sturlson's *Gylfaginning*, but it appears in much more detail in the *Poetic Edda* in a poem called *Skírnismál*, or "The Journey of Skírnir", which focusses on Freyr's servant who travels to Jötunnheim - the land of the Giants -in order to woo Gerðr for his master. The scene begins when Freyr climbs to Hlidskjálf - the high seat of Odin - from which he can see all the worlds. Once there, unfortunately for him and the gods, he becomes entranced by what he sees:

> "A certain man was called Gýmir, and his wife Aurboda: she was of the stock of the Hill-Giants; their daughter was Gerðr, who was fairest of all women. It chanced one day that Freyr had gone to Hlidskjálf, and gazed over all the world; but when he looked over into the northern region, he saw on an estate a house

---

[41] Lindow 2001

great and fair. And toward this house went a woman; when she raised her hands and opened the door before her, brightness gleamed from her hands, both over sky and sea, and all the worlds were illumined of her. Thus his overweening pride, in having presumed to sit in that holy seat, was avenged upon him, that he went away full of sorrow. When he had come home, he spake not, he slept not, he drank not; no man dared speak to him. Then Njördr summoned to him Skírnir, Freyr's foot-page, and bade him go to Freyr and beg speech of him and ask for whose sake he was so bitter that he would not speak with men. But Skírnir said he would go, albeit unwillingly; and said that evil answers were to be expected of Freyr.

"But when he came to Freyr, straightway he asked why Freyr was so downcast, and spake not with men. Then Freyr answered and said that he had seen a fair woman; and for her sake he was so full of grief that he would not live long if he were not to obtain her. 'And now thou shalt go and woo her on my behalf and have her hither, whether her father will or no. I will reward thee well for it.' Then Skírnir answered thus: he would go on his errand, but Freyr should give him his own sword, which is so good that it fights of itself; and Freyr did not refuse, but gave him the sword."[42]

For the details of what Skírnir said next, Sturlson summarizes all too efficiently. Therefore, it's necessary to turn to the Eddic poem, *Skírnismál*, for details of the journey and of Skírnir's methods in "wooing" Freyr's beloved.

"Skirnir spake:
8. 'Then give me the horse | that goes through the dark
And magic flickering flames;
And the sword as well | that fights of itself
Against the giants grim.'

"Freyr spake:
9. 'The horse will I give thee | that goes through the dark
And magic flickering flames,
And the sword as well | that will fight of itself
If a worthy hero wields it.'

"Skirnir spake to the horse:
10. 'Dark is it without, | and I deem it time
To fare through the wild fells,
(To fare through the giants' fastness;)
We shall both come back, | or us both together

---
[42] Gylfaginning 37

The terrible giant will take.'"

Then Skírnir rode into Jötunheim and to Gymir's house, where he found fierce dogs bound before the gate of the fence enclosing Gerðr's hall. Diverted but not waylaid, he rode to where a herdsman sat on a hill. While there, he asks how he can gain entrance into the Gerðr's hall. The herdsman tells him he never shall, but here, the manuscript is incomplete and the poem picks up the story with Gerðr wondering who the stranger is that she hears outside. The result of which is a much simpler invitation to the hall than the herdsman thought possible:

"Gerðr spake:
14. 'What noise is that which now so loud
I hear within our house?
The ground shakes, and the home of Gymir
Around me trembles too.'

"The Serving-Maid spake:
15. 'One stands without who has leapt from his steed,
And lets his horse loose to graze;'
…

"Gerðr spake:
16. 'Bid the man come in, and drink good mead
Here within our hall;
Though this I fear, that there without
My brother's slayer stands.'"

What Gerðr means with this last comment is still debated among scholars, but it's most likely a confused prophetic utterance. Skírnir is not recorded as having killed anybody, whereas his master will, indeed, soon meet Gerðr's brother, Bali. It's likely that Gerðr had some kind of premonition to this effect, and she was merely projecting that onto the messenger.

"Gerðr spake:

17. 'Art thou of the elves | or the offspring of gods,
Or of the wise Wanes?
How camst thou alone | through the leaping flame
Thus to behold our home?'

"Skirnir spake:

18. 'I am not of the elves, | nor the offspring of gods,
Nor of the wise Wanes;
Though I came alone | through the leaping flame
Thus to behold thy home.

19. 'Eleven apples, | all of gold,
Here will I give thee, Gerðr,
To buy thy troth | that Freyr shall be
Deemed to be dearest to you.'

"Gerðr spake:

20. 'I will not take | at any man's wish
These eleven apples ever;
Nor shall Freyr and I | one dwelling find

So long as we two live.’"

Here, Skírnir offers a gift laden with symbolism.
"Golden apples" are a symbol of fruitfulness,[43] an apt gift
from a fertility deity, however, the golden apples referred
to here are most likely those which also bestow eternal
youth. The goddess, Iðunn, was the protector of these
apples and only permitted the gods to eat them, but when
Loki traded them away one time, the gods aged terribly
without them. Therefore, Skírnir is not offering simple
trinkets here—he's offering Gerðr the chance to become
immortal if accepts his hand in marriage. When she
refuses, Skírnir offers one of the gifts made by the same
dwarves that made Gullinborsti and Skíðblaðnir, but there
his patience ends, and he decides to take another tack:

“Skirnir spake:
21. ‘Then do I bring thee | the ring that was burned

Of old with Odin's son;
From it do eight | of like weight fall
On every ninth night.’

“Gerðr spake:
22. ‘The ring I wish not, | though burned it was
Of old with Odin's son;
In Gymir's home | is no lack of gold

---
[43] Bellows 1936

In the wealth my father wields.'

"Skirnir spake:
23. 'Seest thou, maiden, | this keen, bright sword
That I hold here in my hand?
Thy head from thy neck | shall I straightway hew,
If thou wilt not do my will.'

"Gerðr spake:
24. 'For no man's sake | will I ever suffer
To be thus moved by might;
But gladly, methinks, | will Gymir seek
To fight if he finds thee here.'

"Skirnir spake:
25. 'Seest thou, maiden, | this keen, bright sword
That I hold here in my hand?

Before its blade the | old giant bends,
Thy father is doomed to die.

A depiction of Freyr being lovesick

When bribery and violence fails, Skírnir changes direction. What comes next is an example of the magic at which the gods—Odin, in particular—were masters. It takes the form of a physical action (striking with a magic staff), followed by a mixture of curses and ghastly premonitions about Gerðr's fate if she refuses Freyr's advances. The "eagle's hill" mentioned is one such premonition, referring to the hill at the end of Heaven, which overlooks the land of the dead, Hel, where a giant sits in the guise of an eagle, causing the winds to blow when he flaps his ersatz wings. Rather than being comfortable marrying a Giant after the time she spent living amongst them - even a Frost-Giant who was apparently worse than other giants - the prospect of such a marriage is not favorable, though she boasts such an ancestry:

26. "'I strike thee, maid, | with my magic staff,
To tame thee to work my will;
There shalt thou go | where never again
The sons of men shall see thee.

27. 'On the eagle's hill | shalt thou ever sit,
And gaze on the gates of Hel;
More loathsome to thee | than the light-hued snake
To men, shall thy meat become.

28. 'Fearful to see, | if thou comest forth,
Hrimnir will stand and stare,
Men will marvel at thee;

More famed shalt thou grow | than the watchman of the gods!
Peer forth, then, from thy prison,

29. 'Rage and longing, | fetters and wrath,
Tears and torment are thine;
Where thou sittest down | my doom is on thee
Of heavy heart
And double dole.

30. 'In the giants' home | shall vile things harm thee
Each day with evil deeds;
Grief shalt thou get | instead of gladness,
And sorrow to suffer with tears.

31. 'With three-headed giants | thou shalt dwell ever,
Or never know a husband;
(Let longing grip thee, | let wasting waste thee,—)

Be like to the thistle | that in the loft
Was cast and there was crushed.

32. 'I go to the wood, | and to the wet forest,
To win a magic wand;

.   .   .   .

I won a magic wand.

33. 'Odin grows angry, | angered is the best of the gods,
Freyr shall be thy foe,
Most evil maid, | who the magic wrath
Of gods hast got for thyself.

34. 'Give heed, frost-rulers, | hear it, giants.
Sons of Suttung,
And gods, ye too,
How I forbid | and how I ban
The meeting of men with the maid,
(The joy of men with the maid.)

35. 'Hrimgrimnir is he, | the giant who shall have thee
In the depth by the doors of Hel;
To the frost-giants' halls | each day shalt thou fare,
Crawling and craving in vain,
(Crawling and having no hope.)

36. 'Base wretches there | by the root of the tree
Will hold for thee horns of filth;
A fairer drink | shalt thou never find,
Maid, to meet thy wish,
(Maid, to meet my wish.)

37. 'I write thee a charm | and three runes therewith,
Longing and madness and lust;
But what I have writ | I may yet unwrite
If I find a need therefor.'

"Gerðr spake:
38. 'Find welcome rather, | and with it take
The frost-cup filled with mead;
Though I did not believe | that I should so love
Ever one of the Wanes.'

"Skirnir spake:
39. 'My tidings all | must I truly learn
Ere homeward hence I ride:
How soon thou wilt | with the mighty son
Of Njördr a meeting make.'

"Gerðr spake:

40. 'Barri there is, | which we both know well,
A forest fair and still;
And nine nights hence | to the son of Njördr
Will Gerðr there grant delight.'

Then Skirnir rode home. Freyr asked for tidings:

41. "'Tell me, Skimir, | ere thou take off the saddle,
Or farest forward a step:
What hast thou done | in the Giants' dwelling
To make glad thee or me?'

"Skirnir spoke:
42. 'Barri there is, | which we both know well,
A forest fair and still;
And nine nights hence | to the son of Njördr
Will Gerðr there grant delight.'

"Freyr spake:
43. 'Long is one night, | longer are two;
How then shall I bear three?
Often to me | has a month seemed less
Than now half a night of desire."[44]

The *Skírnismál* ends there, but Sturlson picks the story up again in the *Gylfaginning*, making mention of Freyr's fight with Beli. Beli's identity is vague, but he appears to

---

[44] Skírnismál 8ff

be associated with Gerðr and is probably her brother disgruntled by his sister's forced marriage. Sturlson includes a premonition of Ragnarök in this section: "'[Freyr's desire for Gerðr] was to blame for Freyr's being so weaponless, when he fought with Beli, and slew him with the horn of a hart.' Then said Gangleri: 'It is much to be wondered at, that such a great chief as Freyr is would give away his sword, not having another equally good. It was a great privation to him, when he fought with him called Beli; by my faith, he must have rued that gift.' Then answered Hárr: 'There was small matter in that, when he and Beli met; Freyr could have killed him with his hand. It shall come to pass that Freyr will think a worse thing has come upon him, when he misses his sword on that day that the Sons of Múspell go a-harrying.'"[45]

Until this point in the story—and outside of Sturlson's work in general—the character of Beli is entirely unknown, hence the reason for the mystery surrounding him/[46] However, this is not where the mystery of the story ends. Gerðr's etymology and her function as a divinity continue to be debated. It seems very likely that Gerðr performed the function of an "earth goddess" in her own right—although the lights emanating from her hands would suggest she is more connected with the sun—and

[45] Gylfaginning 37
[46] Simek 2007

she formed part of the *hieros gamos*—or "sacred marriage"—alongside her husband, Freyr.[47] Nevertheless, when she marries Freyr, she enters into the Vanir and becomes deeply associated with fertility, too. There is reason to believe Freyr's marriage to Gerðr was an integral part of Freyr's cult, as was the case with fertility deities in the Near East.[48]

   Fertility myths aside, it's likely that this myth can easily be read as an extension of the hostilities between the Æsir and the Giants, or *Jötnar*. More than the dwarves or Dark-Elves, the animosity between the gods and Giants was fervent, insatiable, and most often resulted in the gods depriving their enemies of some treasure or a woman.[49] There is reason to believe the marriage is also indicative of Asgard's hierarchy—whereas the Æsir may take a wife from among the female goddesses who reside in Asgard, the *Ásynjur*, the Vanir must look elsewhere than the Giants where the Æsir look for their concubines.[50]

[47] ibid.
[48] Ellis Davidson 1990
[49] Lindow 2001
[50] Barnes & Ross 2000

Ragnarök

Engravings on the 12th century Urnes stave church believed to depict Ragnarök

One of the most fascinating elements of Norse cosmology is the fact that its end is foretold in crushing detail. This end of times will come about in a mighty battle called "Ragnarök", an event translated as either "the Fate of the Gods" or (in Richard Wagner's re-imagining) "the Twilight of the Gods." Moreover, not only is the event foretold, but the characters of this drama seem to know of its coming. This is in line with the Germanic faith in the concept of "fate." For the German pagans, fate or destiny was an integral part of human existence; while people may not know them ahead of time, their stories are written before they are born, and this was true of the gods as well. Although the gods seem to accept their fates, this concept was not the same as that of "destiny" in Christianity (especially Calvinist pre-destination), because the Norse believed that fate could perhaps be warped and shifted.[51]

With the death of beauty and innocence, the Twilight begins. Then comes the "fimbul winter," three years of endless winter that burden humanity, making the earthly kingdoms battle one another. The bonds that hold the monsters of the world are broken, and Midgard Serpent, Fenris the Wolf, and Loki himself raise an army of giants, monsters and Hell-dwellers to destroy Asgard.

---

51 *The Love of Destiny: The Sacred and the Profane in Germanic Polytheism* (2013) by Dan McCoy, accessed online at: http://norse-mythology.org/wp-content/uploads/2013/03/The-Love-of-Destiny.pdf

The fated end of all things began with the prophecy Odin received and was signaled when all the monsters broke free of their fetters and advanced on Asgard and the gods:

"From the east comes Hrymr | with shield held
high;
In giant-wrath | does the serpent writhe;
O'er the waves he twists, | and the tawny eagle
Gnaws corpses screaming; | Naglfar is loose.

"O'er the sea from the north | there sails a ship
With the people of Hel, | at the helm stands Loki;
After the wolf | do wild men follow,
And with them the brother | of Býleistr [Loki]
goes."[52]

"The Sons of Múspell shall go forth to that field which is called Vígrídr, thither shall come Fenris-Wolf also and the Midgard Serpent; then Loki and Hrymr shall come there also, and with him all the Rime-Giants. All the champions of Hel follow Loki; and the Sons of Múspell shall have a company by themselves, and it shall be very bright."[53]

"Loki shall have battle with Heimdall, and each be the slayer of the other."[54]

[52] Völuspá 50-51
[53] Gylfaginning 51
[54] Ibid.

Naturally, Freyr plays a big role in the coming fight.

"Freyr spake:
41. 'By the mouth of the river | the wolf remains

Till the gods to destruction go;
Thou too shalt soon, | if thy tongue is not stilled,
Be fettered, thou forger of ill.'

"Loki spake:
42. 'The daughter of Gymir | with gold didst thou buy,
And sold thy sword to boot;
But when Müspell's sons | through Myrkwood ride,
Thou shalt weaponless wait, poor wretch.'

"Byggvir spake:
43. 'Had I birth so famous | as Ingunar-Freyr,
And sat in so lofty a seat,

I would crush to marrow | this croaker of ill,
And beat all his body to bits.'

"Loki spake:
44. 'What little creature | goes crawling there,
Snuffling and snapping about?
At Freyr's ears ever | wilt thou be found,
Or muttering hard at the mill.'"

As it turns out, Freyr's "warning" to Loki is actually a
prophecy, since after the *Lokasenna*, Loki is eventually

bound just like his son, though in a much more gruesome manner, as described by Sturlson in the *Gylfaginning*: "[Loki] was taken truceless, and was brought with them into a certain cave. Thereupon they took three flat stones, and set them on edge and drilled a hole in each stone. Then were taken Loki's sons, Vili and Nari or Narfi; the Æsir changed Váli into the form of a wolf, and he tore asunder Narfi his brother. And the Æsir took his entrails and bound Loki with them over the three stones…and those bonds were turned to iron. Then Skaði took a venomous serpent and fastened it up over him, so that the venom should drip from the serpent into his face. But Sigyn, [Loki's] wife, stands near him and holds a basin under the venom-drops; and when the basin is full, she goes and pours out the venom, but in the meantime the venom drips into his face. Then he writhes against it with such force that all the earth trembles: ye call that 'earthquakes.' There he lies in bonds till [Ragnarök]."[55]

Rather than respond with an attack on Freyr, Loki retaliates with a prophecy of his own. The "daughter of Gymir" is, of course, Gerðr, and Loki seems to almost pity Freyr for having sold the sword he knows he will need during the final battle.

Very little is known about Byggvir, the character who comes to Freyr's defense, other than that he was a servant

---

[55] Gylfaginning 49

of Freyr's, along with another, called Beyla. These two characters have been interpreted in many ways by scholars, but they generally tend to agree on some variation of the characters being barley and either cows, beans, or bees.[56]

The Seeress who provides Odin with answers in the 10th century CE poem *Völuspá* gives a brief glimpse of what will come to pass at Ragnarök:

> "Brothers shall strive | and slaughter each other;
> Own sisters' children | shall sin together;
> Ill days among men, | many a whoredom:
> An axe-age, a sword-age, | shields shall be cloven;
> A wind-age, a wolf-age, | ere the world totters."[57]

Sturlson continues the description exquisitely in the *Gylfaginning*:

> "Then shall happen what seems great tidings: the Wolf [Fenris] shall swallow the sun; and this shall seem to men a great harm. Then the other wolf [Hati] shall seize the moon, and he also shall work great ruin; the stars shall vanish from the heavens. Then shall come to pass these tidings also: all the earth shall tremble so, and the crags, that trees shall be torn up from the

[56] Lindow 2001
[57] 45

earth, and the crags fall to ruin; and all fetters and bonds shall be broken and rent. Then shall Fenris-Wolf get loose; then the sea shall gush forth upon the land, because the Midgard Serpent [Jörmungandr] stirs in giant wrath and advances up onto the land. Then that too shall happen, that Naglfar shall be loosened, the ship which is so named. (It is made of dead men's nails; wherefore a warning is desirable, that if a man die with unshorn nails, that man adds much material to the ship Naglfar, which gods and men were fain to have finished late.)…Fenris-Wolf shall advance with gaping mouth, and his lower jaw shall be against the earth, but the upper against heaven, he would gape yet more if there were room for it; fires blaze from his eyes and nostrils. The Midgard Serpent shall blow venom so that he shall sprinkle all the air and water; and he is very terrible, and shall be on one side of the Wolf. In this din shall the heaven be cloven, and the Sons of Múspell ride thence: Surtr shall ride first, and both before him and after him burning fire; his sword is exceeding good: from it radiance shines brighter than from the sun; when they ride over Bifröst, then the bridge shall break, as has been told before. The Sons of Múspell shall go forth to that field which is called Vígrídr, thither shall come Fenris-Wolf also and the Midgard Serpent; then Loki and Hrymr shall come there also, and with him all the Rime-Giants. All the champions of Hel follow Loki; and the Sons of Múspell shall have a company by themselves, and it shall be very bright…

"When these tidings come to pass, then shall Heimdallr rise up and blow mightily in the Gjallar-Horn, and awaken all the gods; and they shall hold council together…Then the Ash of Yggdrasill [The World Tree] shall tremble, and nothing then shall be without fear in heaven or in earth. Then shall the Æsir put on their war-weeds, and all the Champions, and advance to the field …Odin shall go forth against Fenris-Wolf, and Thor stands forward on his other side, and can be of no avail to him, because he shall have his hands full to fight against the Midgard Serpent. Freyr shall contend with Surtr, and a hard encounter shall there be between them before Freyr falls: it is to be his death that he lacks that good sword of his, which he gave to Skírnir. Then shall the dog Garmr be loosed, which is bound before Gnipa's Cave: he is the greatest monster; he shall do battle with Týr, and each become the other's slayer. Thor shall put to death the Midgard Serpent, and shall stride away nine paces from that spot; then shall he fall dead to the earth, because of the venom which the Snake has blown at him. The Wolf shall swallow Odin; that shall be his ending[.] But straight thereafter shall Vídarr stride forth and set one foot upon the lower jaw of the Wolf: on that foot he has the shoe, materials for which have been gathering throughout all time. (They are the scraps of leather which men cut out: of their shoes at toe or heel; therefore he who desires in his heart to come to the Æsir's help should cast those scraps away.) With one hand he shall seize the Wolf's upper jaw and tear his gullet asunder; and that is the death of the Wolf. Loki shall have battle with Heimdallr, and each be the slayer of the other. Then straightway shall Surtr cast fire over the earth and burn all the world…"[58]

Mimir was the Æsir god of wisdom who, after the battles between the Æsir and the Vanir, was sent to the Vanir as a gift of goodwill while the hostages were exchanged. The Vanir felt they had been duped in this "fair exchange," however, and later sent Mimir's head back to the Æsir.

---

[58] 51

When Odin received the head, he embalmed it, placed it in a well beneath the World Tree Yggdrasil (interestingly, on the root that led to Jötunheim), and gave it the power of speech.[59] In order to receive the wisdom from Mimir's head, however, Odin had to give up his eye. Mimir's name is connected with the English word "memory," and Odin's acts in both sending him to the Vanir and ultimately purchasing his wisdom is a common action for the "father god" in myth, the most glaring example being Zeus's swallowing of Metis ("wisdom/cunning") in the Greek tradition.

The "Champions" noted here are the warriors who fell in battle and therefore died nobly in life. Their fate was to be whisked away by the mead-carrying Valkyries to Odin's hall Valhalla (or "Valhöll"). Their fate was to wake up each day and don their armor before fighting each other until the sun fell. Once it did, all of the Champions (or "Einherjar") who fell beneath the weapons of their fellows were resurrected so that they could feast again with Odin that night and drink the never-ending mead that flowed from the udders of the goat Heiðdrun, which grazes on the leaves of Yggdrasil. There is a sense that Odin is "collecting" these heroes in the "mythical present" in preparation of Ragnarök's coming. This is demonstrated in a 10th century court poem called Eriksmál. A

---

[59] ibid.

Norwegian king is killed in battle and the people ask Odin why he chose to take their mighty warrior-king. He responds that the "Wolf" is watching the home of the gods.[60]

48. How fare the gods? | how fare the elves?
All Jötunheim groans, | the gods are at council;
Loud roar the dwarfs | by the doors of stone,
The masters of the rocks: | would you know yet more?

49. Now Garm howls loud | before Gnipahellir,
The fetters will burst, | and the wolf run free
Much do I know, | and more can see
Of the fate of the gods, | the mighty in fight.

Odin's question to the Völuspá is repeated throughout the poem, despite the fact that relatively little is known of the Elves elsewhere.[61] Garmr is a hound that guards the gates of Hel - like Cerberus in the Greek tradition, though there is no evidence of him having three heads - from his "Cliff-Cave" at the entrance to the land of the dead.[62] However, Rudolph Simek suggests that Garmr's conflation with much of the myth of Fenris (his ferocity, fetters and fight against Týr) may have been Snorri's erroneous addition.[63]

---

[60] See Ellis Davidson 1990
[61] Lindow 2001
[62] Bellows 1936
[63] 2007

Nevertheless, Snorri embellishes his account of Loki's child in the Gylfaginning, and the reader can see that the wolf has seemingly never ceased to grow. "Fenris-Wolf shall advance with gaping mouth, and his lower jaw shall be against the earth, but the upper against heaven,--he would gape yet more if there were room for it; fires blaze from his eyes and nostrils. The Midgard Serpent shall blow venom so that he shall sprinkle all the air and water; and he is very terrible, and shall be on one side of the Wolf."

Again, the habitual listener would likely have heard this description with an increasing sense of doom, as it was Thor, their protector, who was fated to fight against the wolf.

50. From the east comes Hrymr | with shield held high;
In giant-wrath | does the serpent writhe;
O'er the waves he twists, | and the tawny eagle
Gnaws corpses screaming; | Naglfar is loose.

Hrymr was the leader of the Giants and this stanza tells the reader the first event that takes place in Jötunheim, namely Hrymr's call to arms. The serpent is the Midgard Serpent, Loki's other child, whose thrashing creates the great waves that will eventually make the land sink beneath them. The "tawny eagle" refers to the giant Hrævelgr, who sits at the edge of the world and causes the winds as he beats his wings.

The stanza leads into the next with one of the eeriest lines in the whole poem.

> 51. O'er the sea from the north | there sails a ship
> With the people of Hel, | at the helm stands Loki;
> After the wolf | do wild men follow,
> And with them the brother | of Býleistr goes.

"Then that too shall happen, that Naglfar shall be loosened, the ship which is so named. (It is made of dead men's nails; wherefore a warning is desirable, that if a man die with unshorn nails, that man adds much material to the ship Naglfar, which gods and men were fain to have finished late.) Yet in this sea-flood Naglfar shall float. Hrymrr is the name of the giant who steers Naglfar."

There is a discrepancy between the Völuspá and Snorri's Gylfaginning. It was generally held that Loki, the "brother of Býleistr" referred to by the Völva, was the helmsman of the Naglfar who drove the dead who had died "ingloriously" (of old age or disease) from their place in Hel (hence "Hel's people"). Loki's ship, Naglfar, made of dead men's nails, became a folkloric mainstay far beyond Iceland by the middle ages. People were warned to cut the nails of their dead as far away as Eastern Europe so as not to give 'the devil' the means of building a ship out of them.[64] The way Loki broke his bonds and arrived on

Naglfar is not revealed in the existing sources. Nevertheless, Loki's etymology likely foreshadowed the closing of the era of the Norse gods, which would place him as a key figure at the beginning of Ragnarök,[65] and his role as a trickster implies the inevitability of his escape. All tricksters, whether through changing their shape or being rescued by some heroic figure, slip the traps made for them. It is how they learn and how they advance as characters, and the trap itself often only serves as a narrative device to create tension before the inevitable escape comes. Loki was the force of chaos in the world and given chaos' unavoidable existence in the world as almost an act of hubris on the part of the gods who tried to bind him. In all myths, tricksters slipping traps are often given apocalyptic importance, and, in terms of Loki, he is the cause of the end of the cosmos and the pantheon as they were known.[66]

> "In this din shall the heaven be cloven, and the
> Sons of Múspell ride thence: Surtr shall ride first,
> and both before him and after him burning fire; his
> sword is exceeding good: from it radiance shines
> brighter than from the sun; when they ride over
> Bifröst, then the bridge shall break, as has been
> told before.

---

[64] Simek 2007
[65] ibid.
[66] Hyde 2008

"The Sons of Múspell shall go forth to that field which is called Vígrídr, thither shall come Fenris-Wolf also and the Midgard Serpent; then Loki and Hrymrr shall come there also, and with him all the Rime-Giants. All the champions of Hel follow Loki; and the Sons of Múspell shall have a company by themselves, and it shall be very bright. The field Vígrídr is a hundred leagues wide each way."

The "Sons of Múspell" come from a region that had a connection with the beginning of the cosmos. According to Norse tradition, at the beginning there was a vast void called the "Ginnunga gap." Into this void flowed an icy cold from the region of Niflheim - the "dark world" - and sparks and embers from the land that was "hot and bright", Muspellsheim. It's likely that the leader of this fiery realm was Múspell, and therefore his "horde" that broke the bridge that connected Asgard to Midgard would have Surtr as a fitting leader.[67]

This is reference to the fire giant Surtr, whose "sword is exceeding good." Surtr does not appear on any of the stone carvings that have survived into the 21st century, but there is a theory that he represents a peculiarly Icelandic mentality that influenced Ragnarök greatly. As a so-called "fire giant" some scholars (like Ellis Davidson) have

[67] Lindow 2001

written that he was a "Volcano Demon." Volcanoes are still dominant natural features in Iceland, whose flames and billowing clouds of ash continue to "blot out the stars" today. The effect of these natural surroundings on the writings of the Ragnarök stories appears to have been considerable. Comparing accounts of the terrible volcanic eruption in Laki, Iceland, in 1783, Ellis Davidson suggests the "sequence of events was the same as in the Völuspá: first earthquake tremors shook the mountains, then the sun was darkened by clouds of smoke and ashes, then came blazing flames, with smoke and steam while the melting ice caused serious flooding by water as well as by burning lava; if we add a tidal wave from the sea to this series of catastrophes, the situation is very close to that in the poem."[68] Given that one of Iceland's volcanoes, Hekla, erupts on average every 35 years, imagining Iceland as the birthplace of the mythology that attributes the birth and death of all things to meetings of extreme heat and extreme cold does not seem so far-fetched.

From a literary standpoint, and to the habitual listener of this story, the mention of Surtr in the above passage would have also been a warning bell for the end of one of the gods. As recorded in the Lokasenna, Freyr gave up his magical sword in favor of his love for a giantess, and it was against Surtr's magical sword that he would

---

[68] 1990

eventually meet his death. Weapons play a very important part in the Norse myths and in the Norse (and even Anglo-Saxon[69]) mindset. They were as much a part of the individual as an arm, they often received names, and, in the case of Thor's hammer Mjölnir, they came to represent a protective force for the community. It's a necessary point to understand since contemporary listeners of the story may well have wondered what might have happened had Freyr not abandoned this magical and formidable weapon before it was needed at Ragnarök.

An illustration depicting the fight between Freyr and Surtr

[69] see Ellis Davidson

The name given to the battlefield, Vígrídr, has excited many scholars in the past due to its connections or similarities to the biblical Armageddon. Originating from the name of an artificial mound in modern-day North Israel, "Tel Meggido" was the site of several famous and bloody battles from as early as the 15th century BCE and became the nexus of a series of forts that were built to protect the key trade route that passed through the vast plain. This connection with a vast plain on which countless lives have been lost no doubt turned into the apocalyptic "myth-place" in the Book of Revelation, but most scholars today believe the similarities between the biblical and Norse battlefields to be little more than coincidence given new life by later Christian writers.

> 53. Now comes to Hlin [Frigg] | yet another hurt,
> When [Odin] fares | to fight with the wolf,
> And Beli's fair slayer | seeks out Surt,
> For there must fall | the joy of Frigg [Odin].

"Odin rides first with the gold helmet and a fair birnie, and his spear, which is called Gungnir. He shall go forth against Fenris-Wolf …The Wolf shall swallow Odin; that shall be his ending but straight thereafter shall Víðarr stride forth and set one foot upon the lower jaw of the Wolf: on that foot he has the shoe, materials for which have been gathering throughout all time. (They are the scraps of leather which men cut out: of their shoes at toe or heel; therefore he who desires in his heart to come to the Æsir's help should cast those scraps away.) With one hand he shall seize the Wolf's upper jaw and tear his gullet asunder; and that is the death of the Wolf."

The "yet another hurt" line here refers to the death of Baldr, for whom Frigg tried so hard to protect. There's an interesting correlation between Baldr and his father's deaths; it was Loki who convinced Hödr to throw the mistletoe at his brother, and Loki was the father of the wolf that left Frigg a widow.

An illustration depicting Odin and Fenrir, with Freyr and Surtr in the background

Víðarr's story contains the same kind of folkloric elements as that of Naglfar, mentioned above.[70] Whether being prudent with their toenails or deliberately throwing away scraps of leather, the average person could "come to the Æsir's help." The interesting part of this story is that there is very little known of Víðarr elsewhere in the surviving literary works. He doesn't appear in the skaldic poetry outside the Eddas, which means it's likely that he was a literary invention for later purposes.[71] This may explain the confusion between Fenris and Garmr to some extent, as it would make much more sense for Týr to fight the taker of his hand than for him to die at the maws of Hel's hound.

"Thor shall put to death the Midgard Serpent,
and shall stride away nine paces from that spot;
then shall he fall dead to the earth, because of the
venom which the Snake has blown at him."[72]

56. In anger smites | the warder of earth,--
Forth from their homes | must all men flee;-
Nine paces fares | the son of Fjorgyn,
And, slain by the serpent, | fearless he sinks.

The Völuspá reveals here that Thor is the "Warder of Earth," and this was no small role for the contemporary readers/listeners. Unlike Eggther, who was mentioned at the onset of the battle as "warder of the Giants" and, as

---

[70] Simek 2007
[71] ibid.
[72] Gylfaginning 51

such, more like a counterpart to Heimdall,[73] Thor's role was as "protector" of gods and men. Oaths were sworn on his hammer, Mjölnir, and there are extant moulds that suggest the likeness of Mjölnir was worn around the neck as a form of protection, just like the Christian cross.[74] Thor is the son of Fjorgyn in this account, too, though elsewhere he is referred to as the son of Earth and Odin.

A runestone in Sweden depicting Thor's hammer

[73] Simek 2007
[74] Ellis Davidson 1990

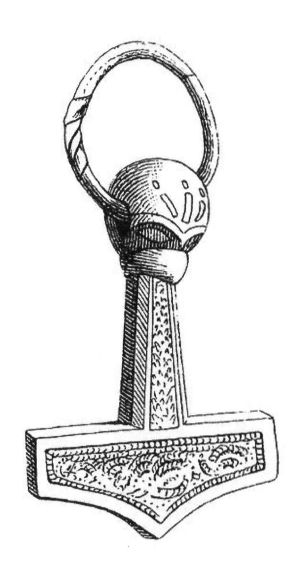

**Drawing of an amulet of Thor's hammer found in
Denmark**

An illustration depicting Thor and the Midgard Serpent

Nevertheless, Thor dies in a truly mythological way by fighting a monster. Gods against monsters is a vital theme to Ragnarök, but it is also a universal theme in world myth, as Simek points out: "Indra fights against Vrtra, Apollo against Python."[75] It isn't out of mythological neatness that this story survives, as there may be a Christian element that contributed. The Old Testament monster Leviathan became equated with the Midgard Serpent after the Christianization of Scandinavia. Just as Thor once baited the Midgard Serpent with the Giant Hymir's best Oxe's head, so in the Old Testament was Leviathan baited with Behemoth.[76]

---

[75] 2007
[76] ibid.

The connection between Leviathan and the Devil and the bait and Christ, according to Rudolph Simek, led these two myths to converge and influence each other to the point that depictions of the Midgard Serpent were found on the Christian cross at Gosforth, and later translations of the term "Midgard Serpent" and its name "Jörmungandr" translate directly to "Leviathan". Christ, the defeater of the "Leviathan" and savior and protector of the world, was not difficult to equate with the "warder of the gods" then.

The fates of Freyr and Týr are excellent examples of how the events of Ragnarök are connected with events and actions of the earlier stories. This is not as common as it may seem, either. The surviving sources assert that Loki and Heimdall battle to the death at Ragnarök but no surviving story shows that they held particular animosity towards each other, nor that their actions had created this inevitable duel.[77]

In the case of Freyr and Týr, however, their conflict is inevitable. Týr was the god who fed Fenrir and placed his hand in the wolf's mouth as collateral for any trickery the gods might have in mind. He was the one-handed god after this event, and it would have been understandable if Týr and Fenrir battled to the death. However, as the following passage from the Gylfaginning shows, this was

---

[77] ibid.

not the case. "Garmr [the Hound], which is bound before Gnipa's Cave: he is the greatest monster; he shall do battle with Týr, and each become the other's slayer."

Týr's lies actually resulted in his name being connected with perjury in medieval Iceland, and this may be the key to understanding why Fenris killed Odin instead of Týr. Odin was considered to be devious, and, unlike the strength and hammer of Thor, lies were a major part of Odin's arsenal. There is an interesting etymological connection between Týr and Odin that might have further conflated the two. Týr is connected with the Indo-European root-word meaning "deity" in general and Sigtýr, meaning "Victory Týr/Deity", was one of the many names Odin went by. There is much speculation among scholars of mythology as to the formation of pantheons and etymology often reveals earlier prominence of a god or goddess that is later seen as subordinate to another, such as Poseidon and Zeus. If this is the case in the Norse myths, and certain scholars believe it to be so, then the Fenrir's motivation to slay the progenitor of lies rather than the liar himself would make perfect sense. Little else is said of Garmr's animosity towards Týr but being another monstrous canine may have been reason enough to have him battle the victim of Fenrir.

Freyr's fate was, accidentally or not, prophesied by Loki in the Lokasenna. While insulting the gods, Loki launches a reminder at Freyr of how he gave up his famed magical sword in order to marry a woman, and a Giant at that. His demise appears in the Gylfaginning in the following passage: "Freyr shall contend with Surtr, and a hard encounter shall there be between them before Freyr falls: it is to be his death that he lacks that good sword of his, which he gave to Skírnir ..."

An interesting point mentioned by John Lindow is that Freyr was known for his ability to fight without a sword, as he did against the giant Beli, whom he killed with an antler. This may be the reason behind the line in the Völuspá that states Freyr sought Surtr even without his sword. Perhaps there is some missing prophecy or rationale behind Freyr's defeat, but, for now, scholars must simply accept that it was prophesied by the Völva for the "mythic future" and the results would be thus:

> 57. The sun turns black, | earth sinks in the sea,
> The hot stars down | from heaven are whirled;
> Fierce grows the steam | and the life-feeding flame,
> Till fire leaps high | about heaven itself.

A depiction of the final scene of Ragnarök

An illustration depicting the new world after

Ragnarök

The beginning of the post-Ragnarök world starts in stanza 59 of the Völuspá, with the Völva looking into the future and recording what she "sees" for Odin:

> 59. Now do I see | the earth anew
> Rise all green | from the waves again;
> The cataracts fall, | and the eagle flies,
> And fish he catches | beneath the cliffs.

> 60. The gods in Ithavoll | meet together,
> Of the terrible girdler | of earth they talk,

> And the mighty past | they call to mind,
> And the ancient runes | of the Ruler of Gods.

Stanza 59 has often been quoted to show the influence of Christianity on Norse religious belief,[78] and while that is subject to debate, what cannot be debated is that nearly all surviving written accounts of Norse myths were written by Christians.[79] In fact, prior to the conversion to Christianity, the Norse myths were still part of a predominantly oral tradition. It was only with the Christian tradition of manuscript writing that these myths came to be recorded.[80] Thus, to the acolytes of Norse religion, the written word was a sacred thing. The "Ruler

---

[78] Bellows 1936
[79] Lindow 2001
[80] ibid.

of Gods" here is Odin, and the runes were his because it was he who brought them to mankind after hanging from the World Tree, Yggdrasil, for nine nights.

The survivors of Ragnarök go to Ithavoll - the "field of deeds" that is not mentioned anywhere else other than in this stanza[81] - and discuss the things of old, including the runes and the spells they invoked, and the old gods and the monsters they battled, such as the Midgard Serpent, the "terrible girdler of earth." Like the fireside raconteurs and the Lawspeakers at the "Thing," the new age is welcomed and understood by the storytellers of memory, without whom the myths of Ragnarök and the "Old Gods" would not have survived.

61. In wondrous beauty | once again
Shall the golden tables | stand mid the grass,
Which the gods had owned | in the days of old,

.   .   .   .

62. Then fields unsowed | bear ripened fruit,
All ills grow better, | and Baldr comes back;
Baldr and Hoth dwell | in Hropt's battle-hall,
And the mighty gods: | would you know yet more?

63. Then Hönir wins | the prophetic wand,

.   .   .   .

---

[81] Bellows 1936

And the sons of the brothers | of Tveggi abide
In Vindheim now: | would you know yet more?

There is a beautifully cyclical nature apparent in these stanzas that is inherent in all Norse mythology. The "fields unsowed" that bear ripened fruit and all "ills" being alleviated are typical of post-apocalyptic paradises, but the return of various characters is striking here. Baldr, the "best" of the gods whose death Loki affected through the hand of Hoth, comes back to life and, along with his brother and unwitting murderer, lives in Odin's "battle-hall" of Valhalla. Fratricide was a particularly intractable situation for a culture such as that in medieval Iceland. Blood-feuds were used to settle disputes within the society, but a brother killing another brother would have unavoidable and unlimited repercussions that could not be resolved by a third-party.[82] Therefore, having the two brothers unite and live peacefully in Valhalla is a sign of a new age of peace and tranquillity.[83]

As for the rest of the gods in this stanza, very little is known of Hönir other than being present with Odin and Loki in a few episodes, and that he was given the gift of prophecy for the new age. The line "sons of the brothers of Tveggi" needs to be unraveled, but the results are unsatisfying. Tveggi is another name for Odin, and his

[82] Lindow 2001
[83] Bellows 1936

brothers were Vili and Vé, with whom Odin killed the primeval Giant Ymir and created the world. Sadly, nothing is known of their sons other than that they would preside over the new from the golden hall of "Gimle".

> 64. More fair than the sun, | a hall I see,
> Roofed with gold, | on Gimle it stands;
> There shall the righteous | rulers dwell,
> And happiness ever | there shall they have.

In the Vafþrúðismál - the verbal duel between Odin and Vafþrúðnir, the wisest of all Giants - the post-Ragnarök age is elaborated on beautifully. After greeting each other and declaring their wisdom as their weapons, they battle to the death by questioning the knowledge of the other. Beginning at the point in which Odin finally questions the giant about how he came to acquire such a vast amount of wisdom, Vafþrúðnir's answer provokes a sudden change in Odin. Until this point, Odin had begun each question with a number and the line "answer me well | if thy wisdom avails," but not so from here on:

> Odin spake:
> 42. "Twelfth answer me now | how all thou knowest
> Of the fate that is fixed for the gods;
> Of the runes of the gods | and the giants' race
> The truth indeed dost thou tell,
> (And wide is thy wisdom, giant!)"

Vafþrúðnir spake:

43. "Of the runes of the gods | and the giants' race
The truth indeed can I tell,
(For to every world have I won;)
To nine worlds came I, | to Niflhel [Niflheim] beneath,
The home where dead men dwell."

From here on, Odin takes the upper hand in the duel. He reminds the Giant that he too has traveled far, and that he too has discovered many things, including those secrets of the gods that most will never know. In the Codex Regius, the Vafþrúðismál comes after the Völuspá, and if the reason for this ordering is based on more than just the stylistic whim of the Codex's compiler, then Odin's introductory lines to his questions would appear to refer to the things he found out from his interrogation of the Völva.

Odin spake:

44. "Much have I fared, | much have I found,
Much have I got of the gods:
What shall live of mankind | when at last there comes
The mighty winter to men?"

Vafþrúðnir spake:

45. "In Hoddmimir's wood | shall hide themselves
Lif and Lifthrasir then;

The morning dews | for meat shall they have,

Such food shall men then find."

Very little is known of the humans that re-populate the earth. Snorri quotes this stanza in his Gylfaginning and wrote that they will have a vast amount of children, but aside from this description, the recorders of Norse myths tend to have given Lif and Lifthrasir little attention in their manuscripts.[84] They survived the "awful winter" in "Mímir's Treasure (Hodd)". Generally speaking, this "wood" is thought to be the World Tree Yggdrasil, which was watered by Mímir's well.[85] Mímir's head dwelt in this well near one of the roots of Yggdrasil and there is some evidence of a tree called "Mímameid" nearby, which many believe to be just another name for Yggdrasil.[86] Nevertheless, these beings would be protected from the Fimbulwinter, survive the shaking of Yggdrasil and the end of the gods, and be nourished on the dew that gathered in the World Tree's leaves.

Odin spake:
46. "Much have I fared, | much have I found,
Much have I got of the gods:
Whence comes the sun | to the smooth sky back,
When Fenrir has snatched it forth?"

Vafþrúðnir spake:

---

[84] Lindow 2001
[85] Bellows 1936
[86] ibid.

47. "A daughter bright | Alfrothul bears
Ere Fenrir snatches her forth;
Her mother's paths | shall the maiden tread
When the gods to death have gone."

This is an excellent example of the confusion between the surviving sources. According to the Völuspá, it isn't Fenrir who steals the sun but his son Sköll.[87] This could be generously interpreted as "the father being the cause of his son's actions" but that would entail an ultimately untenable stretching of the familial cords. Snorri calls Alfrothul "Elfin-Beam" when he quotes this stanza at the closing of the Gylfaginning, and her birth is another of the cyclical aspects of Ragnarök. She is not only as beautiful as her mother but chooses to take up the same path she trod to bring illumination back to the world.

It appears there was a reason for the recording of Ragnarök by the Christians, and some historians believe it was documented because it bears many resemblances to the Christian apocalypse, thus serving as an easy transitional story for contemporary believers of Norse mythology to better understand their new religious situation. Joseph Campbell marked the similarities between the Norse and Christian "End Times" by citing the Gospel of Matthew: "Immediately after the tribulation of those days shall the sun be darkened, and the moon

---

[87] ibid.

shall not give her light, and the stars shall fall from heaven, and the powers of the heavens shall be shaken. And then shall appear the sign of the Son of man in heaven. And then shall all the tribes in the earth mourn, and they shall see the Son of man coming in the clouds of heaven with power and great glory."[88]

This is not definitive proof of Christianity's influence on the Norse myths, but the ending of both the Vafþrúðismál and the Völuspá have given scholars plenty to think and argue about for the past few decades.

One of the most interesting stanzas to this effect comes out of the Völuspá, but only the version found in the Hauksbók.

> 65. There comes on high, | all power to hold,
> A mighty lord, | all lands he rules.
>
> . . . .
> . . . .
>
> 66. From below the dragon | dark comes forth,
> Níðhöggr flying | from Nithafjoll;
> The bodies of men on | his wings he bears,
> The serpent bright: | but now must I sink.

The ending to the Völuspá is confusing in many ways. First, stanza 66 appears to be an incongruous addition to

---

[88] see Campbell 2008

this part of the story. Aside from the last half line, where the poem ends with the Völva suddenly saying that she must sink into the earth, the rest of the stanza would look more at home earlier on during the battles between the gods.[89] Some people have suggested that this passage was inserted here to give the sense of evil's tenacity, as the dragon that gnawed the roots of Yggdrasil, Níðhöggr, rises from the depths to try one last time to vanquish the powers of good. What is clear is that it comes after an obvious allusion to the Christian belief system that does not fit with the rest of the poem, despite the presence of similarities between the two traditions.

The stanza does not appear in the Codex Regius at all, which has led to some translators rejecting it or including a lacuna beneath, as Henry Adams Bellows did in the version quoted above. Bellows noted that in some late paper manuscripts, the lacuna is filled with two other spurious lines: "Rule he orders, | and rights he fixes, Laws he ordains | that ever shall live."[90]

These late additions to the poem (if they do indeed refer to Christianity) could be seen as a marker of contemporary belief in a kind of "divine chronology." The idea that the Christian God arrived in Scandinavia after those of the Æsir and Vanir was commonly taught during

[89] Bellows 1936
[90] ibid.

the period in which Christianity became the dominant religion in the region (10th and 11th centuries CE). In some aspects, this would help establish a relatively smooth takeover by Christianity, but there is evidence to suggest that there was a sense of "rivalry" between Christ and the "Warder of the Earth" Thor. Indeed, it seems as though the "old gods" had to be defended by Snorri Sturlson from those who would dismiss them as "demons" and their stories as the work of the Devil. Stanza 65 may well have been written into the poem as a result of this kind of "Norse apologetics" by Christians, and the choice to place it at the end of the story of Ragnarök (and even to have preserved the story in the first place) tied in with the Christian view of the "divine chronology."

Axel Olrik also analyzed the similarities of the descriptions in the Völuspá and those of the Bible and found that the "moral state of the world," the sounding of the apocalyptic horn Gjallarhorn, (with the trumpet of Gabriel) the sun's disappearance, Surtr's all-consuming fire, and the description of the new world all coincide with the worldview according to the Gospel of Matthew and Revelations in the Bible.[91] Faced with these similarities, and the euhemeristic approach to understanding Norse myths that was popular at the time, later Christians most likely came to see Ragnarök as the end of the gods and

---

[91] see Simek 2007

people's worship of them.[92]

H. R. Ellis Davidson, however, disagrees with those who would see the ending of the poem as representative of the poet's original intention to show the "triumph" of Christianity over the old religion. If this had been the case, the rest of the poem would no doubt have been much more explicit. If the idea of Ragnarök were nothing more than a simple import from the Christian tradition, then more allusions to the Christian God would be expected throughout the Völuspá. The possibility a Christian writing to exist at that time with such unabashed freedom to describe the old gods is very unlikely. Even Snorri Sturlson, a Christian, made sure to include a "warning" in the prologue to his Edda for other Christians who might fall into the trap of believing in such stories as the literal truth of the divine cosmos. No such warning is even hinted at in the Völuspá.[93]

That these stories presaged the oncoming Christian God is a tempting theory but unlikely, not least of all because the Scandinavian storytellers had their own gods in mind for the new world. The last question Gylfi asks in Snorri's Gylfaginning is "Shall any of the gods live then, or shall there be then any earth or heaven?" Hárr gives the following answer:

---

92 Lindow 2001
93 Ellis Davidson 1990

"Víðarr and Váli [Odin's vengeful sons] shall be living, inasmuch as neither sea nor the fire of Surtr shall have harmed them; and they shall dwell at Ida-Plain, where Ásgard was before. And then the sons of Thor, Módi and Magni, shall come there, and they shall have Mjölnir there. After that Baldr shall come thither, and Hödr, from Hel; then all shall sit down together and hold speech. with one another, and call to mind their secret wisdom, and speak of those happenings which have been before: of the Midgard Serpent and of Fenris-Wolf. Then they shall find in the grass those golden chess-pieces which the Æsir had had; thus is it said:

  'In the deities' shrines | shall dwell Víðarr and Váli,
    When the Fire of Surtr is slackened;
Módi and Magni | shall have Mjölnir
    At the ceasing of Thor's strife.'"

Apparently, the writer of the Völuspá seems to have had access to a lot of pre-Christian sources on Ragnarök. There are glimpses of them in poems dating back to the 9th century CE, and there is even a memorial stone inscription found in Skarpaler, Sweden that has been interpreted as "Earth shall be torn asunder, and high heaven." Ellis Davidson reasonably points out that "a scholar's theory from a foreign source is not likely to find its way on to a gravestone" that was not a Christian one. Depictions of what are believed to be Ragnarök themes on gravestones and crosses, such as those on the Gosforth Cross in Cumbria, are fairly common throughout northern England and the Isle of Man from the 10th century CE onwards, when the Viking settlers would have had well-established communities in the area. This material evidence has been used to support the argument that Ragnarök was born out of a larger and earlier body of traditional stories that were not influenced by Eastern cultures.

Thus, Davidson suggests that viewing the poem as the progression from "the Old to the New" does not do the mythology justice. Despite the similarities to the biblical Armageddon, the story of cosmic destruction and resurrection is part of the greater tradition of world myth. The return of goodness to the world after a cataclysmic event is present in religions as disparate as those of the Abrahamic tradition, Hinduism, Buddhism and Zoroastrianism. In the latter belief system in particular, there are striking similarities. For example, there is a winter akin to that of the Fimbulwinter, and there are warnings against disposing of nail cuttings carelessly "lest they should be used by the forces of evil."[94] There is little reason to believe that even the Celtic battle between the

---

[94] Ellis Davidson 1990

gods and giants, their own "Twilight," was simply the result of borrowing from the Norse tradition, either, as some historians suggested in the past. The ideas prevalent in the Völuspá are typical of how humans have imagined their demise and cosmic doom for millennia, and within those stanzas there is a human unity that is at once fascinating and touching.

Perhaps one of the most notable aspects of Norse mythology is that, unlike many of the other belief systems humans have created over the millennia, the gods are destined to fall from their benighted and hallowed positions. As a result, a lot of people believe Ragnarök is the end. What is less often made clear in the story of Ragnarök is the cyclical view of the cosmos that comes out of the floods and fires. It embodies a special mindset that the medieval Scandinavians possessed; they accepted that evil exists and will no doubt get the upper hand on many occasions, yet there is always the possibility of a new day, a sentiment that is far from bleak.

Freyr's story ties in to the actual history of the region and how it affected Norse mythology. His story is one of contrast, whether it's between peace and war, life and death, or lust and love. Since he wasn't an Æsir, it is likely the Christians who transcribed the Norse myths did not see him or his deeds as particularly relevant to their endeavor. The contrast between the mythic dramas and his presence in a temple dedicated to Odin and Thor, his license to sit in Odin's exalted chair looking over the worlds, and the importance of his cult (as evident in the archaeological record) is what makes Freyr an interesting a character to study. The fact so little is known about the stories of his "life" makes historians curious as to why he was so widely and fervently worshipped. At the same time, it leaves scholars wondering what stories have been lost because they were not written down or because they were written on the kind of materials that did not survive.

 Thankfully, there is enough in the archaeological record and in the records from other cultures with similar fertility deities to make an educated guess concerning the prestige Freyr demanded, even amongst the Æsir. Freyr's connection with the sun and fertile earth are two reasons why Freyr's devotees were remembered long after they had gone for the devotion freely given to him. Although his worshippers in the far western reaches of Scandinavia may not have been as numerous as those of other gods, Freyr was certainly one they would want to idolize. Who, after all, would be the most welcome visitor in the bleak, frigid lands of Northern Europe than a god who promised abundance, marriage, children, and the cessation of violence so common amongst the gods and the tribes of mankind alike?

Online Resources

Other books about mythology by Charles River Editors

Bibliography

Barnes, G., and Ross, M.C., (2000) *Old Norse Myths, Literature and Society* Sydney

Bellows, H. A., (1936) *The Poetic Edda* Evinity Publishing inc

Brodeur, A. G., trans (1916) *Snorri Sturlson's Prose Edda* The American Scandinavian-Foundation, New York

Campbell, J., (2008) *The Hero with a Thousand Faces* New World Library

De Vries, J., (1933) *The Problem of Loki* Folklore Fellows FF Communications, Helsinki

Dumézil, G., (1965) *Gods of the Ancient Northmen* University of California Press

Eliade, M., (1971) *The Myth of the Eternal Return: Or, Cosmos and History* Princeton University Press

Eliade, M., (2004) *Shamanism: Archaic Techniques of Ecstasy* Princeton University

Ellis Davidson, H. R., (1990) *Gods And Myths of Northern Europe* Penguin Books

Faulkes, A., trans. (2012) *Snorri Sturlson's The Uppsala Edda* Viking Society for Northern Research, University College London

Frazer, J. G., (1922) *The Golden Bough* Macmillan

Grimm, J., (2012) *Teutonic Mythology* Cornell University

Hyde, L., (2008) *Trickster Makes This World: How Disruptive Imagination Creates Culture* Canongate Books

Laing, S., trans (1844) *Snorri Sturlson's Heimskingla, or The Chronicle of the Kings of Norway* London

Lindow, J., (2001) *Norse Mythology: A Guide To The Gods, Heroes, Rituals And Beliefs* Oxford University Press

Morris, W., trans (1888) *Volsunga Saga* Walter Scott Press

Radin, P., (1956) *The Trickster: A Study in American Indian Mythology* Knopf Doubleday Publishing Group

Richards, J., (2005) *The Vikings: A Very Short Introduction* Oxford University Press

Simek, R., (2007) *Dictionary of Norse Mythology* D. S. Brewer, Cambridge

Turville-Petre, G., (1964) *Myth and Religion of the*

North: The Religion of Ancient Scandinavia. New York: Holt, Rinehart and Winston

Free Books by Charles River Editors

We have brand new titles available for free most days of the week. To see which of our titles are currently free, click on this link.

Discounted Books by Charles River Editors

We have titles at a discount price of just 99 cents everyday. To see which of our titles are currently 99 cents, click on this link.

Made in the USA
Monee, IL
10 April 2023

31645530R00059